Other Books About Children by David Heller

The Best Christmas Presents Are Wrapped in Heaven
(with Elizabeth Heller)

Grandparents Are Made for Hugging
(with Elizabeth Heller)

Fathers Are Like Elephants Because They're the Biggest Ones Around
(But They Still Are Pretty Gentle Underneath)

My Mother Is the Best Gift I Ever Got

Love Is Like a Crayon Because It Comes in All Colors

"Growing Up Isn't Hard to Do If You Start Out as a Kid"

Mr. President, Why Don't You Paint Your White House Another Color!

Talking to Your Child About God

Dear God: Children's Letters to God

Dear God, What Religion Were the Dinosaurs?

The Children's God

Just Build
the Ark
and the Animals
Will Come

Just Build the Ark and the Animals Will Come

Children on Bible Stories

David Heller

Villard Books
New York 1994

Library of Congress Cataloging-in-Publication Data
Heller, David.
Just build the ark and the animals will come: children on Bible
stories/by David Heller.
p.   cm.
ISBN 0-679-42756-2 (alk. paper)
1. Bible stories, English—O.T.   2. Children—Quotations.
3. Children—Religious life.   I. Title.
BS551.2.H445   1993
221.9′505—dc20   93-29963

Manufactured in the United States of America on acid-free paper
9 8 7 6 5 4 3 2
First Edition

With Love and Reverance
for God

"Out of the mouths of babes
You have sent wisdom . . ."*

*This interpretation of Psalm 8 is from *A Child's Bible*.

Acknowledgments

I want to express my gratitude and affection for the hundreds of children who participated in my study and whose lively comments and beliefs appear in this book. What a joy it was to meet them and get to know them. They taught me so much about religion and life in general. And what a diverse group they were, as they represented an incredible variety of religious backgrounds. The children were Catholic, Jewish, Lutheran, Episcopalian, Muslim, Christian Scientist, Greek Orthodox, Baptist, Humanist, Unitarian, Methodist, nondenominational Protestant, interfaith, religiously unaffiliated, and many other different religions.

I also want to thank their parents, teachers, and principals, as well as their schools and houses of worship, for taking me in and allowing me time with their youngsters. I particularly want to thank the Archdiocese of Greater Boston for their extensive help. Also, I wish to acknowledge Dan Connolly, a wonderful teacher and a good friend of mine, for his ongoing help with my books.

This book was born out of my sudden brainstorm and a subsequent meeting with my publisher and editor, Diane Reverand. Perhaps it is fitting that our meeting took place on Good Friday/Passover weekend of 1992. I want to express my appreciation for Diane's partnership in our publishing ventures and for her steady guidance and insight concerning the children and the content of my books.

My wife, Elizabeth, is ever a part of all my books and a wonderful consultant on children. I am grateful to God for her presence in my life and in my work.

In many ways, I was in training for this book during most of my life. In addition to the religious outlook of my parents, which was clearly formative for me, I was influenced by my early Hebrew school days at Shaare Torah in Bridgeport, Connecticut, and then by a strong Jesuit influence at Fairfield Prep in Fairfield, Connecticut. Later, at Harvard, I was fortunate to take such courses as "The English Bible," taught by the late Bible scholar Morton Bloomfield, and then, at Michigan, I studied under and became friends with Professor of Psychology and Religion Richard Mann who guided my dissertation on children and religion.

Background research was also an important element of this book. Along with reviewing and reading several Bibles, I found the following books to be invaluable: *Bible Stories from the Old Testament,* Linda Hayward, ed. (New York: Grosset and Dunlap, 1987); *The Tall Book of Bible Stories,* Katherine Gibson, ed. (New York: Harper & Row, 1957); *A Child's Bible,* Anne Edwards, ed. (London: Puff Publishers, 1967); and *The Old Testament Story* by John Drane (New York: Harper & Row, 1983). More recently, the talks of the Reverend Ina Warren on "Demystifying the Bible" were also an excellent resource.

To all these individuals and works, I am deeply grateful.

Contents

Introduction

This is a book about children's views of the Bible, one of the great classics if not the grandest collection of books ever written. The Bible is no ordinary masterpiece; many people believe it is inspired by God. Certainly, we can all agree that it contains half of the history of civilization, extending as it does from remote antiquity to about two thousand years ago. Remarkably, the Bible is the centerpiece of many diverse religions and is the principal prayer book for millions and millions of people around the world today.

The Bible consists of sixty-six books, of which thirty-nine make up the Old Testament (excluding some disputed books, called the Apocrypha) and twenty-seven the New Testament. This library of books is not simply a descriptive account of the world, but an unparalleled array of history, law, poetry and wisdom, prophecy, philosophy, epic stories, and drama. While the Bible is full of thought-provoking ideas and intellectual substance, it is fundamentally intended to be inspirational and spiritually practical. The Bible is a teaching book and a guideline for living, inviting all readers to embrace righteousness and the ways of God through faith in God's goodness and glory.

For this particular project, youngsters from many different religions focused on the best known Bible stories from the Old Testament. The first of the two testaments chronicles the creation of the world, the first trials and tribulations of man, the history of the Jewish people, and the omnipotence of God and the wisdom of God's laws. Most of the Old Testament was probably written between 1400 and

400 B.C. Initially passed along in the Jewish oral tradition, and then later written down by assorted writers, the Old Testament claims among its likely authors the legendary Moses, the kings David and Solomon, and the prophets Samuel and Isaiah—the latter was the prophetic voice who foretold the coming of a messiah. We are uncertain about the authorship of numerous Old Testament books, but we do believe with some certainty that most of it was originally scribed in Hebrew.

The prevailing message of the Old Testament is subject to each believer's interpretation, but we might summarize the consensus view in this way: the world is not just a random thing but the design of the One True God. Man can have a real and personal relationship with God, though too often evil and sin on man's part interfere with the relationship. While God does punish wickedness, God is a loving and forgiving God who offers people salvation if they learn from their mistakes and learn to trust in God's divine wisdom.

With this underlying theme, the Old Testament reveals God's ways through the good times and bad times of Adam and Eve, the terrible Flood and the Ark that God protected, the early lineage of the Chosen People, tyranny and slavery in Egypt, Moses the redeemer and the Exodus story, life in the Promised Land, further captivity, and the adventures of colorful Bible figures like Samson, David, Daniel, Jonah, and Job. But there are plenty of adversaries too. Whether the antagonist is the Serpent in the Garden, Pharaoh, Delilah and the Philistines, Goliath, an enormous whale, a den of lions, or Satan himself, God is always there for the people, and God never lets them down. Each biblical story is at once history and morality play, and each offers essential and timeless lessons for both children and adults.

Now, the child's view of the Bible, and the Old Testament in particular, tends to be humorous and lighthearted, and yet it is unmistakably full of faith. "Laughter," said the theologian Reinhold Niebuhr, "is the beginning of prayer." That is the abiding theme of our approach to the Bible. What a delight it is to witness the child's wonder and curiosity about fantastic scenes like the Garden of Eden or the animals assembling two by two in front of Noah's Ark, and to laugh with joy along with youngsters as they argue the pros and cons of wrestling with an angel. Yet, observing how children grapple with serious issues of right and wrong, faith and sin, and good and evil is equally enlightening. In the same breath, children may entertain us and still teach us about the nature of our existence and about the nature of God.

Our purpose is to celebrate the Bible by means of a lively journey with children through their favorite Old Testament stories. The stories, and the youngsters who attempt to tell them, remind us of a basic, down-to-earth wisdom we all need. And this also provides us with a wonderful opportunity to see the world and the Bible through the eyes of a child—eyes brimming with hope and faith and love for a God that is beyond the scope of our imaginations and yet can be readily found in a child's heart, and in our own hearts as well.

—David Heller, Ph.D.

I

"In the beginning God was lonely, so He made people to play with"

(the story of Creation)

The Creation story is the elemental story in all of Western culture, and it holds a special and magical place in the minds of children. The idea that great heavenly bodies and an entire planet could emerge out of vast emptiness may be difficult to comprehend, but that makes Creation all the more wondrous and ripe for the youthful imagination. Children do have some very vivid notions about the origin of things—and that includes their ideas about the earth, the sun and the stars, the first people, and, above all, the Lord God, who made it all come to be.

"In the Beginning . . ."

"In the beginning, God scratched His gray hair, rolled up His sleeves, and decided to get down to work and make Himself a nice world."
Andrew, age 12

"In the beginning, God had some big ideas. . . . One of them was round and had a lot of blue and green on it and some big humps called mountains."
Heather, age 10

"God created heaven and earth, but that didn't make Him too busy to spend time with His children."
Robert G., age 8

"God made the moon and the light. Then the electric company took over, but that wasn't until many years later."
Bart, age 9

"In the beginning, the sky needed a lot of work but it wasn't easy for God because He had a bad back."
Andrea, age 7

"In the beginning God was lonely, so He made people to play with. . . . You could talk to them better than you could talk to dinosaurs."
Teri, age 7

The Essential Thing That God Created on the First Day of Creation

"Pizza . . . with extra cheese."
Corinne, age 6

"I would say it was air was created on the first day. Air was one of His toughest creations because He couldn't see it while He was making it."
Wendy, age 10

"Love was created on the first day, and the rest is history."
Nancy Z., age 11

"Stars . . . so Eve could write 'Twinkle, Twinkle, Little Star' when she got older."
Elizabeth T., age 6

"Light and a pair of sunglasses for Himself because the sun was brighter than He was figuring."
Terry B., age 8

~~~

"Heavens and earth and less important stuff like rain."
Jerold, age 8

The Famous Words of God as He Blessed All of the Creatures of the Sea and Sky

~~~

"Good morning, Earth! Blessed are My creatures because they are perfect. . . . I don't have a big ego or anything, it's just that these birds and fish really did come out perfect."
Andi, age 8

~~~

"Some of you are going to be able to fly and some aren't, but I don't want you to get jealous of each other."
Millie, age 9

~~~

"Tweet! Tweet! Tweet! That has a nice ring to it."
Taylor, age 8

~~~

"Shalom, birds and fish. I hope you have a good life."
Carey, age 7

On Why the First Man, Adam, Was Created Before the First Woman, Eve

≈≋≈

"Adam had to be first so He could build the house and have it ready before Christmastime."
Roland, age 8

≈≋≈

"Handsomeness before silliness."
Greg, age 11

≈≋≈

"God was more sure of how the man would look, but ladies were still a mystery to Him."
Grant, age 8

≈≋≈

"God had to wait for her because He hadn't invented makeup yet."
Janice, age 9

≈≋≈

"God was going in alphabetical order. . . . Adam was an *A*."
Elizabeth C., age 8

≈≋≈

"It's because God is a She and She wanted to get Adam out of Her hair already. He was a nuisance in heaven."
Diana, age 12

"The first person had to be stronger so he could protect them from wild horses and cantaloupes."
Herb, age 7

≈

"God was experimenting to begin with. Then God got it right when He made women."
Lacy, age 9

The Unusual Circumstances of How Eve Was Created

≈

"She was created out of dust. Adam and Eve were dust products."
Fred, age 9

≈

"Just don't tell me it was the stork. I'm not believing that."
Dick, age 7

≈

"Was her mother the Virgin Mary too?"
Robin, age 8

≈

"God took Adam's rib and made Eve from it, but that probably left Adam wonderin' if some other part of him was next."
Tyrone, age 10

"She got made from a bone. Do you know what her first words were? She said, 'Where is that lamebrain husband of mine? C'mere, husband!'"
Anita D., age 9

The Controversy over Why God Created Women

"It was just for laughs."
Darrell, age 11

"The world needed a woman's touch."
Leandra, age 10

"To take care of little people like me."
Nick, age 5

"It was basically to go shopping."
Cassie, age 7

"God wanted to make the world as colorful as possible, and Adam just didn't look that good in pink."
Anita D., age 9

"So there would be two sexes and two groups. Then you could go off with your group and go hunting together or play board games."
Carey, age 7

"After Adam, if God had just created another man, Adam and the other guy would have just thrown a football around all day and they would have got nothing done."
Damon, age 9

"Ladies were created to be partners and sometimes they should be the ones that make the decisions . . . except when it comes to fruit and trees."
Rob, age 12

Various Explanations for Why God Required Rest on the Seventh Day

"He needed a mental health day."
Peggy, age 10

"His toes were aching Him."
Herb, age 7

"I think it was because he wanted to have one big day set aside for sports."
Mike, age 8

"He had to spend some time with His wife."
Ally, age 6

"God needed time to think. What was the best way to make millions of people on the earth? The Eve-from-Adam's-rib way was too hard."
Millie, age 9

"He was exhausted from creating. Creating is hard because you have to decide a lot of different things and that takes a lot of energy. . . . I get tired too when I'm creating something."
Carey, age 7

"God had to go to church on that day. So He put aside His work and prayed for a long time. . . . God prays for all the people and all the animals too. He wants everything to work out okay."
Neal, age 7

If There Had Been an Eighth Day of Creation, the Other Things That God Might Have Done

≈≈

"He might have hired somebody to do the weather because that's too much for one person to watch over."
Josh, age 6

≈≈

"Take away the thing He created called a 'temper.'"
Lauren, age 12

"Adam tasted Eve's apple because he was just a man in love"

(the Garden of Eden story and the first family)

he epic story of mankind's time in paradise, and his equally famous fall from grace, is passed on through the Bible to each and every generation. Regardless of our individual personal beliefs, there is no disputing the richness of the characterization and the power of the morality play that the Garden drama conveys. Adam and Eve and the nefarious serpent, and, later, Cain and the ill-fated Abel, are all captivating in their simple yet profound roles—each a study for reflection. For children, Eden is particularly fascinating, a world from long ago where everything was just perfect, at least until man and woman, through their own curiosity and rebellion, were forced to abandon the Garden and forge a life for themselves. Children have their own ideas about what exactly went wrong and what the Garden of Eden story teaches us.

Differing Opinions About What the Garden of Eden Was Really Like

"It only had one tree but it sure was a whopper."
Roland, age 8

"The oranges were as big as basketballs. . . . They had to use an ax to cut them in half."
Larry G., age 9

"It was sunny all the time, with plenty of palm trees to sit under and a little stream that was something like a whirl-pool. . . . Eve liked to go in there and relax."
Vickie, age 11

"It wasn't as good as you would think. They didn't have any toilet paper back then."
Russ, age 10

How Adam and Eve Spent an Average Day in the Garden of Eden

"I think they did yoga most days."
Joanna, age 11

"They played tag. It was simple enough to learn. Even a snake could play."
Krista, age 8

≈≈≈

"Probably they took long walks in the new moonlight that God had created and tried to figure out what to do about loneliness. That's when they decided to have the first children."
Craig, age 12

≈≈≈

"They drew pictures of God and colored them in with crayons they made out of vegetables. . . . Most of the pictures of God came out green."
Catherine, age 8

≈≈≈

"Adam and Eve played bingo and the churches picked up on it later on."
Peggy, age 10

≈≈≈

"They had deep talks about what they were there for. . . . People have been trying to figure that out ever since."
Jerome B., age 9

≈≈≈

"Adam and Eve wanted to go on a trip to heaven, but God told them they couldn't travel. So they just camped out on earth and made the best of it every day."
Jefferson, age 8

On What Adam and Eve's Marital Relationship Was Like

≈≈

"I'm not even sure they even got married, but nobody ever talks about that."
Carey, age 7

≈≈

"They found themselves stuck together in that Garden home so they just had to make the best of it. . . . They realized that marriage ain't all roses and kissing—it's got problems with snakes in it too."
Mary, age 11

≈≈

"It was rough at first but God was a good marriage counselor."
Wendy, age 10

The Fundamental Rule That God Put Forth to Adam and Eve About the Garden

≈≈

"THE BIG TREE TREE IS SACRED. DON'T MESS WITH IT."
Terry N., age 11

"NO SMOKING, NO DRINKING, NO LATE PARTIES, AND DON'T BUILD ANY IDOLHEADS!"
Connie, age 10

≈

"NO TRESPASSING BY SATAN. . . . If you happen to run into a fellow that goes by the name of the Devil, tell him you you're in a hurry and you can't talk to him. . . . Then give him My card."
Vickie, age 11

≈

"STAY AWAY FROM TALKING SERPENTS. . . . They are big-mouth troublemakers."
Doug, age 8

≈

"REMEMBER TO SAY A BLESSING OVER THE FOOD YOU EAT. . . . It might help it to taste better, which will come in handy when you get to liver."
Lewis, age 11

≈

"DON'T HIDE FROM ME WHEN I COME VISIT YOU. . . . There's no reason to be scared of Me. I'm a gentle God."
Yvonne, age 7

What Was the Serpent's Real Motive in the Garden Story?

≈≈≈

"Nothing too deep. The serpent just wanted Adam and Eve out of the neighborhood because they were nudists."
Danny, age 9

≈≈≈

"Souls. . . . He was in the soul-stealing business."
Edgar, age 12

≈≈≈

"The serpent was just trying to stir up a little action because nothing much happened in the Garden since Creation."
Porter, age 8

≈≈≈

"He was just a troublemaker. . . . He liked to get God upset and give God indigestion."
Dick, age 7

≈≈≈

"The snake wanted to get famous and he couldn't figure out a healthy way to do it. . . . This way he knew people would be talkin' about him for centuries."
Alec, age 9

What Precisely Did the Serpent Say to Eve to Convince Her to Take That Fateful Bite of the Forbidden Apple?

~~~

"It's okay to taste the apple, Eve. . . . It's low-calorie."
Celia, age 11

~~~

"See this diamond jewelry, Eve. I'll give it to you at a discount
if you try the apple just once."
Connie, age 10

~~~

"Look, lady, if you eat the fruit snack God isn't really goin' to
do nuthin'. . . . God is just a big bluffer. Trust me."
Bart, age 9

~~~

"You know, Evie, you aren't getting any younger. . . . Apples
help you to look like you are still young. Think of it as a
health product."
Johnny, age 9

~~~

"This is yummy fruit and so sweet. It's high in vitamin C and
you can't eat only one. Mmmm, good!"
Carey, age 7

"I'll tell it to you straight. Would you rather have these nice apples for dinner or slave over a hot cooking fire? It's your choice."
Peggy, age 10

≈

"Don't listen to God. He's on a power trip."
Anita D., age 9

≈

"You can be as smart as God. But hurry! Act fast! It's a limited offer."
Heather, age 10

What Made Adam Go Along with Eve and Taste the Forbidden Fruit?

≈

"When a wife says it's good for you, the husband usually follows."
Carey, age 7

≈

"Eve had pretty eyes and she was batting them pretty good."
Anita D., age 9

≈

"Adam tasted Eve's apple because he was just a man in love. . . . They're always supposed to act silly and foolish."
Alissa, age 8

"Adam was starving and Eve wouldn't make any dinner if Adam didn't go along and eat the silly fruit."
Thomas J., age 8

The Punishments That God Handed Out as a Result of the Tree of Knowledge Incident

"No more Garden parties."
Millie, age 9

"They couldn't have apples or applesauce for a week."
Beth, age 5

"I don't know exactly what He did with the people, but He turned that snake into a real creepy crawler!"
Karl, age 9

"Adam and Eve were afraid that God was going to turn them into fish, but instead, they just got turned into average working people."
Damon, age 9

"The man was going to have to be a cropper all his life and the lady would have to be a housewife. . . . That was until women got liberated."
Jeb, age 9

≈≈≈

"They had to hunt for their food. The food didn't just come to them and give in."
Nicholas, age 7

≈≈≈

"There was a big sword blocking the Garden and a big yellow sign that said: DO NOT ENTER ANYMORE. THAT MEANS YOU, ADAM AND EVE!"
Eugene, age 9

≈≈≈

"Adam and Eve had to leave that Garden neighborhood, but we're going to get back there one of these days. . . . I have faith in that."
Gabriel, age 10

What Kind of Parents Did Adam and Eve Turn Out to Be After They Left the Garden of Eden?

≈≈

"Adam and Eve were the type of parents who wanted their children home before darkness was created."
John L., age 12

≈≈

"Bad role models. . . . They didn't listen to Higher Authority."
Geoffrey, age 12

≈≈

"Pretty much primitive. . . . They probably spanked their kids too much for small things, like naming oceans after themselves."
Heather, age 10

≈≈

"Pretty poor parents. . . . No discipline in that oldest kid. . . . The one named Cain."
Alec, age 9

What the Brothers Cain and Abel Were Actually Upset Over That Ultimately Led to Abel's Death

≈≈

"Abel stole Cain's dinosaur cards."
Jamelle, age 7

≈≈

"Who had more boulders in his collection."
Art, age 10

≈≈

"Abel was upset because Cain was an atheist, which was pretty weird in those days since God was around a lot on a regular schedule."
Frannie, age 8

≈≈

"Cain felt that Able was the one God liked better, but he was wrong. . . . God doesn't play favorites."
Peggy, age 10

When God Asked Cain About What Happened to Abel, What Was Cain's Famous Reply?

"Abel who?"
Neal, age 7

"My brother? Alive or dead? Is this a multiple-choice question?"
Celia, age 11

"I'm not my brother's keepsake."
Vickie, age 11

"I want to see my lawyer before I answer any more questions, God."
Johnny, age 9

"I am innocent until proven guilty. . . . What do you mean this isn't a democracy? What kind of world are you running, Mr. God?"
Shannon, age 8

"Abel slapped me first. . . . You know, an eye for an eye, a head slap for a head slap. You know how it is, right?"
Jocelyn, age 11

The Lasting Punishment That God Gave Cain

≈≈

"Cavities."
Augie, age 7

≈≈

"For the rest of his life, he had to look and act like a nerd."
Dean, age 10

≈≈

"Wanderer city, man."
Jason, age 10

≈≈

"He had to travel all around and stay in strange places where they didn't have king-size beds."
John C., age 8

≈≈

"No girlfriends. . . . I don't know if he ever got a wife, but that's different. It don't count as fun."
Howie, age 8

"Cain would forever be a bad guy in the book that God was writing."
Cal, age 9

What Can We Learn About Brothers from the Story of Cain and Abel?

"Brothers should be nice to each other for religious reasons."
Ellyn, age 6

"Remember to treat people like friends, not brothers."
Rob, age 12

"Don't be upset with things you don't have. It leads to jealousy and life on the road."
Connie, age 10

"Stick with competing in basketball. . . . It's much more safe."
Emilio, age 7

"Don't let evil feelings get the best of you. Try to remember that it was just yesterday or the day before that you were just playin' together and having fun together."
Sandy, age 10

"Just build the Ark and the animals will come"

(Noah's Ark and the great flood and much, much more)

ew Bible stories captivate children as much as the saga of Noah and his famous Ark. While the prospect of a wicked world destroyed by a great flood could well intimidate young children, the vision of those cooperative animals lining up two by two for the classic nautical journey entertains and fascinates the youngsters. They take considerable delight in imagining what life on the Ark was like for those forty days and forty nights. How did the people and animals get along? What did they all do during the long voyage? Such questions are the springboard for much lively speculation and childhood theorizing.

Then, as the children ponder the miraculous rainbow and the new beginning for the Earth, they offer symbolic interpretations for all of us to share. Through their jocular views of the Ark story and its spiritual symbolism, the children help us to understand that we are irrevocably linked to nature and, of course, to our Creator, bound as we are by human needs and our love for each other.

Why God Became Wrathful Toward the People of the Earth as the Years Passed

≈≈≈

"They bowed down to idols during idol time."
Carey, age 7

≈≈≈

"Bad prayers, or no prayers or at all."
Lori Ann, age 8

≈≈≈

"Too much sinning and too much sex stories in the newspapers."
Dean, age 10

≈≈≈

"The citizens weren't energy conscious enough."
Lena, age 9

≈≈≈

"Mostly, it was like the people were lost sheep and they lost their way."
Robin, age 8

Why Was Noah Chosen as the Builder of the Ark and the Survivor of the Great Flood?

〜〜

"Noah was in the navy and he knew a lot about ships."
Demetrius, age 7

〜〜

"Noah was a nice guy. . . . Who says that nice guys finish last?"
Glenn, age 11

〜〜

"That Noah person had connections. He knew a couple of angels personally."
Carmen, age 8

〜〜

"Noah was a leader. He had a loud voice, so the animals would listen to him when he told them to get up on the boat fast because it was starting to rain."
Joe, age 8

The Special Instructions That God Gave to Noah with Regard to the Ark and the Big Journey at Sea

"Don't hammer too loud. You'll wake up the heavens."
Peggy, age 10

"Just build the Ark, Noah, and the animals will come. . . .
Trust me."
Brett, age 11

"No, Noah, you can't take your exercise equipment with you on
the Ark. This isn't a pleasure trip!"
Natalie, age 10

"Make it holy. Put a Jewish star that lights up on the outside
and make it an eternal light."
Carey, age 7

"There is no batteries included with this Ark. . . . So some
assembly may be required, Noah."
Gil, age 12

How Did Noah and His Family Keep Busy on the Ark for Forty Days and Forty Nights?

"They held three- and four-legged races."
Georgio, age 9

"The same things as they do on the Norwegian Carnival boats you see on TV, except they couldn't stay outside and get tans."
Christopher, age 10

"The family did something easy like Scrabble, and the animals played polo."
Roberta, age 8

"The boys just kept imagining when they could play baseball again. They hoped the season could be scheduled again after all the rain-outs."
Dick, age 7

"The Noah family took a crash course in animal rights. . . . They had to because they were outnumbered."
Bernadette, age 12

"There was even a special room for prayers. When the rain started, even the wild animals like leopards kneeled down and prayed."
Penny, age 7

How Did Noah First Discover That the Waters Had Dried Up Enough for a Landing?

〜〜

"God left a sign that said: READY FOR LANDING, NOAH. PARK THE BOAT RIGHT HERE. GOD."
Jeb, age 9

〜〜

"Whenever the ship bumped into the shore and knocked everybody down, then it was time to land."
LeToya, age 11

〜〜

"A rainbow that was shaped like an arrow pointed to where the land was."
Emilio, age 7

〜〜

"Noah hit a golf ball and it landed in a sand trap."
Cody, age 12

"Noah sent a dove out and the dove brought back a
branch. . . . From then on, the branch means that there is going
to be peace in the world."
Carey, age 7

What Did the Rainbow Symbolize for God in His Communication with Future Generations?

"That God was a supporter of drawing and the arts."
Clare, age 10

"A rainbow is a celebration in heaven. When it rains, God is
crying and when it thunders, God is yelling at the angels. But
a rainbow is more like a holiday."
Sheila, age 9

"It showed that God liked creating things more
than He likes to destroy them. He don't like that at all, but
sometimes He has to."
Reid, age 7

"Rainbows always mean: 'Everything is going to be okay from
now on.' "
Janet, age 10

When They Were Finally off the Ark, What Were the First Words of Noah and Family?

"Thank God we don't have to do this every year!"
Barry, age 10

"Those animals weren't so bad after all. . . . Let's remember to send them Christmas cards."
Christine, age 10

"That rainbow was pretty. . . . I hope it doesn't have to rain again for forty days and nights before we can see it again."
Anita V., age 7

And the Generations of Noah Begat New Generations, and There Were People on the Earth Again—But Why Did They Build the Giant Tower of Babel?

〰️

"To put a nice restaurant right there up at the top floor
of the tower."
Barry, age 10

〰️

"To explore the sky and see if it was really blue close up, and
to see if they could move the clouds around so they could
control the weather or at least predict it."
Millie, age 9

〰️

"Those generations thought you had to be high and mighty to
be religious. . . . They didn't know that you just have to be
nice and friendly."
Cal, age 9

〰️

"I think they wanted to check out heaven in person. . . .
But heaven was a lot higher than the thirtieth floor."
Sandy, age 10

What Happened to the People After They Built the Tower?

≈≈≈

"When God arrived on the scene, the people all got tongue-tied
. . . so to speak."
Mitch, age 11

≈≈≈

"They couldn't understand each other anymore, so they had to
talk with their hands. That's why a lot of people still do that."
Gayle L., age 10

≈≈≈

"The tower fell like it was made of Legos."
Keith C., age 11

≈≈≈

"God scattered the people across the whole world. . . . But it
didn't end up all bad, because it created a lot of different
cultures and languages. And someday we're going to all get
back together."
Gerard, age 11

IV

"Abraham, make me an altar, and make it snappy!"

(the story of Abraham and the early days of the Chosen People)

And it came to pass that God chose a man named Abraham to be the first Jewish person and start the first monotheistic religion. *Monotheistic?* That sure is a big word for children. They may not know what it means, but they do sense the importance of early religious figures as the foundation of the modern belief in a single God. They are generally aware of who Abraham was, have heard of the great paternal dilemma surrounding the near-sacrifice of Isaac, and have even acquired some knowledge of those pillars of civilization, Sodom and Gomorrah. Well, sort of. Even when some of the biblical detail is sketchy, the young scholars make absolutely certain that they are capturing the abiding spirit of the Good Book.

And they are not too young or naïve to comprehend that lessons about faith and sin are revealed through these stories. You can be assured of that.

When God First Spoke to a Man Named Abraham, What Difficult Thing Did He Tell Him to Do?

≈≈

"Change his name and become a spy."
Gayle B., age 8

≈≈

"Start a religion without a priest or minister or rabbi. . . . It's hard to do it because the people will be expecting a big talk at the service, or else they won't feel like they did their duty."
Maura, age 9

≈≈

"God said to him, 'Abraham, make me an altar, and make it snappy!' "
Jerome M., age 10

≈≈

"Maybe it was to become the first Jewish person to start leadin' them to the Promised Land. . . . Maybe it was something about not eating pigs."
Bernadette, age 12

≈≈

"He had to change his name from Abra to Abraham. . . . That was going to be his stage name."
Dennis, age 12

"Abraham had to figure out how to make people believe in a God they couldn't see or touch. . . . It was a tough job but somebody had to do it."
Sara L., age 9

When You Are Beginning a New Religion Like Abraham Was, What Kind of Things Do You Have to Consider?

"Make sure some of the people don't think they are holier than some of the others. . . . That's always a lot of trouble."
Christine, age 10

"What prayers you should chant. . . . And remember to keep 'em short, or else you will lose a lot of the people who are following you."
Cody, age 12

"When to call something a miracle. . . . If you are wrong, everybody will think you're a phony."
Maura, age 9

"Abraham probably wasn't preachy. He probably just led by being an example. You should do that too."
Dean, age 10

～～

"Make sure the religion is all about love. . . . Those are the religions that last the longest."
Sara L., age 9

The Miraculous Event That Happened to Abraham and His Wife Sarah When They Were in Their Nineties

～～

"They got to be on a first-name basis with the Man Upstairs."
Barry, age 10

～～

"When Abraham and Sarah were in their nineties, they learned how to waltz."
Kim N., age 12

～～

"God took away all their wrinkles."
Anita D., age 9

"Abraham and Sarah got married. They were the oldest people to ever get married. . . . It was because they had to be sure."
Glynnis, age 7

"Abraham became the father of Isaac. . . . Which was pretty incredible because Abraham was one ol' dude and Sarah was no teenager either."
Michael, age 11

On Why Sarah Is Said to Have Laughed All the Time Prior to the Birth of Isaac

"Abraham was always tickling her and bringing her pickles."
Doug, age 8

"Her doctor was a real kidder. . . . She thought he was kidding until the baby came out."
Toni, age 11

"She was happy that God was letting her get pregnant, just like he helped Mary a lot of years later."
Maura, age 9

"She was in a good mood because she was pregnant and her husband was waiting on her for a change."
Peggy, age 10

≈

"She bought funny baby announcements with angels and trumpets on 'em and she couldn't wait to pass them out."
Mary, age 11

What Was the Famous Way That God Tested Abraham's Faith?

(Hint: It Involved His Son, Isaac)

≈

"Abraham had to change Isaac's diapers to prove how much love he had for him."
Shannon, age 8

≈

"God made Isaac really sick and so Abraham had to trust a doctor to fix him, but it was really against his better judgment."
Christine, age 10

≈

"Abraham and Isaac were told to go out and walk on water. . . . But then they found out that this was for really big names like Jesus."
Sandy, age 10

"Abraham was supposed to sacrifice his son on an altar. . . . In modern times the fathers don't have to do that. That's why there is so many sons around."
Troy, age 8

What Do You Think God Was Trying to Demonstrate by Telling Abraham to Sacrifice his Son?

"You should love your son. . . . He could be the only one you got."
Herb, age 7

"Have faith in God. He won't let you down even if it doesn't all add up at first."
Liz, age 10

"Listen to what God says. He gets you going in the right direction. You just gotta have faith that it will work out in the end."
Albert, age 8

"God don't want crazy sacrifices. . . . Just love and a little nice prayers to Him will do."
Irene, age 7

Now, It Came to Pass That Some of Abraham's Relatives, Including Nephew Lot and His Wife, Lived in Two Towns Named Sodom and Gomorrah. . . . What Kind of Towns Did These Turn Out to Be?

"Once God got through with them, they were pretty much ghost towns."
Albert, age 8

"For the most part, they were like average American towns."
Virginia, age 9

"Something like Los Angeles."
Owen, age 10

"The kind of places with a lot of problems. . . . They might've even had too much dirt."
Herb, age 7

"Exciting towns where a guy could get in a lot of trouble. . . .
Too bad they aren't around no more."
Derrick, age 8

"They were sinners who deserved what they got. . . . They got
smooshed."
Barry, age 10

As a Result of Some Fancy Negotiating by Abraham, What Were the Conditions under Which God Would Have Spared Sodom and Gomorrah?

"Extra taxes sent straight to Heaven."
Alex, age 10

"Abraham had to promise to be good and he couldn't say
things to God like 'Jeezus, what to you expect from me?' "
Bernadette, age 12

"Those towns had to do better about recycling and the
environment."
Joyce, age 9

≈

"The Sodom and Gomorrah people had to want to become a
democracy and they had to have elections by some date on
their calendar."
Robin, age 8

What Happened to Lot's Wife, the Tragic Relative of Abraham, When She Disobeyed and Looked Back at the Destruction of Sodom and Gomorrah?

≈

"She did a big wipeout."
Andrew, age 12

≈

"Didn't she turn into a sand castle or something?"
Maura, age 9

"She got the worst case of acne anybody ever saw."
Gayle B., age 8

~~~

"Lot's wife turned into a pillar of salt. . . . That just about killed their marriage right there."
Keith G., age 11

V

"Joseph's coat of all those colors was a hand-me-down, and I wouldn't have taken it if I was him"

(about the patriarchs Jacob and Joseph, the famous coat present, and how both father and son found a lot of meaning in dreams)

he biblical patriarchs Jacob and Joseph stand out as strong and exemplary family figures who continue the tradition of belief in a single God. But their unique adventures also make them exciting characters for children, as the youngsters imagine what it would be like to see some angels ascending a ladder and then wrestle with one, or wear the world's most beautiful coat and also be able to interpret God's spiritual messages.

Jacob is most noted for his wilderness escapades and for his pivotal tussle with an angel of God. The Bible tells us how Jacob became the father of a great nation, as his offspring became the twelve tribes of Israel.

Joseph, one of the sons of Jacob, is beloved for two things: his famous multicolored coat and his knack for interpreting dreams. Oh, that dazzling coat! Think of all the difficulties it caused Joseph. It practically cost him his life, and it did cost him his freedom; but, on the other hand, it was all part of his chosenness, as God had selected him for great things.

Children are quite familiar with brother problems, and they have seen a fancy coat or two, but these exotic biblical dreams are a whole other thing altogether. Can dreams really predict the future, and, as such, are they veiled messages from God? The kids are curious and they share their personal views along with their rich and endearing accounts of Jacob and Joseph.

What Did Jacob, the Son of Isaac, Dream About While He Was Sleeping on a Stone in the Wilderness?

"Harem ladies."
Liz, age 10

"He was dreamin' about a ladder that went to heaven. I think he was going to climb up on it, but then he figured: 'Wait a minute. I like it here on earth. I think I'll stay.'"
Jimmy C., age 12

"There was a bunch of angels playing cards. . . . You know how dreams are kinda silly, but there's always a message in them?"
Lena, age 9

With Whom Did Jacob Wrestle in the Wilderness?

"It wasn't Hulk Hogan, that's for sure. . . . I don't even know if Hulk has a religion."
Richard, age 10

"A lion . . . but Jacob won. . . . It wouldn't have made sense if he lost, because then they would have to end the story right there."
Laurie, age 9

"An angel that was passing through on the highway to heaven."
Barry, age 10

"I think he might have been wrestling with God. God was just doing it to see if Jacob had what it takes to be in charge of the Holy Land."
Cal, age 9

Why Was This Wrestling Match Such an Important Turning Point in Jacob's Life and in the History of His People?

"He knew he must have been picked to do something important. He figured the angel wasn't just picking a fight with him just to keep in shape."
Robert G., age 8

"He was called 'Israel' from then on. . . . It meant he would be the new leader and they would have a country with plenty of fruit and funny huts there."
Gabriel, age 10

≈≈

"Jacob proved he was worthy of God's attention. . . . God doesn't like to take big chances, especially when the guy he is betting on is going to be big in the whole religion later on."
Andrew, age 12

≈≈

"Jacob wrestled with an angel so he could get the biggest halo when he got to heaven."
Sheri, age 9

In Time, How Many Sons Did Jacob Have, and Why Did This Number Become Significant?

≈≈

"Were they Catholic? . . . It could be a lot."
Shauna, age 9

≈≈

"A dozen kids. . . . It was significant because it started people selling eggs in that number. . . . Just fooling. I think it was twelve so they could start the twelve tribes of Israel."
Larry K., age 12

"It was about twelve. One for each month. Probably the child born in February was the shortest."
Robin, age 8

≈

"I don't know how many there were, but I think one of them was a little one named Joe."
Dick, age 7

Concerning How the Son Named Joseph Acquired His Coat of Many Colors

≈

"There was a sale at the Israel Department Store."
Sara F., age 11

≈

"Was it for Hanukkah?"
Marian, age 7

≈

"He found it in some bushes. It said PROPERTY OF MICHAEL JACKSON on it."
Greg, age 11

≈

"He got it from his parents for getting A's in Bible school."
Jill, age 8

"I know it was supposed to be so pretty, but I bet Joseph's coat of all those colors was a hand-me-down, and I wouldn't have taken it if I was him."
Virginia, age 9

Because the Coat Made Them So Jealous, What Did the Other Sons of Jacob Do to Young Joseph?

"Did they get him in trouble with his teacher?"
Francis, age 7

"They threw him down a well to see if he would bounce. . . . Joseph didn't bounce."
Dean, age 10

"They made him eat stale oatmeal."
Augie, age 7

"They sold him to Pharaoh's servants for something like fifty bucks and one of those sundial watches."
Keith C., age 11

While He Was Imprisoned in Egypt, What Special Ability Did Joseph Begin to Demonstrate?

"He could juggle while he was praying."
Ricky, age 7

"He could talk to animals. . . . It was popular then like doctors and lawyers are today."
Wendy, age 10

"He was good with dreams and he made a fortune doing fortune-telling."
Terry N., age 11

"His special thing was psychic visions. . . . He could have been on *Unsolved Mysteries*."
Kristen, age 12

How Do You Think Joseph Got to Be So Good at Interpreting Dreams?

"Joseph slept ten hours a night, so he had plenty of experience on his own dreams."
Liz, age 10

"I think all his brothers had the special power for it too. They were like a dream team."
Doug, age 8

"His secret was going to bed early. That's when the messages come to you from Heaven."
David, age 8

"God sorta told him what the meaning was by talking to him in a special voice. . . . Joseph and the other Bible people, they knew it was God because the voice was real strong and gentle and full of truth too."
Andrew, age 12

When He Was Summoned to Pharaoh's Court, What Did Joseph Say About Pharaoh's Dream of the Fat Cows and the Thin Cows?

≈

"Pharaoh, the moral of this dream is that you have to watch your weight.
Clare, age 10

≈

"He told the Pharaoh: 'Sir, only use thin cows in the royal dairy because thin cows can give you one-percent milk."
Darlene, age 11

≈

"On no, Pharaoh. It means a famine is coming. Better eat your Wheaties and store up a lot of food right now!"
Craig, age 12

≈

"My great Pharaoh, here is what I think. We are going to have seven good years and seven bad years. Somebody must have broke a mirror and that's why we are getting the bad luck."
Sally, age 11

Like Joseph, Do You Believe That All Dreams Are Sent from Heaven and Have Some Special Meaning in Them?

"Mine are sent by God. . . . I can't say for you."
Becky, age 8

"Definitely no. Last week I had a dream where a killer plant ate my nine-year-old brother. . . . That one probably wasn't sent from heaven."
Art, age 10

"Good dreams are sent by God but dreams about teachers yelling are sent by the Devil!"
Terry B., age 8

"I think many dreams are from God because sleep is when God does His most important work."
Lori Ann, age 8

What Did Joseph (Now Pharaoh's Special Minister) Say to His Hungry Brothers When They Came into the Palace to Purchase Grain?

"Hello, Brothers! How is it going? It's time to even the score for selling me as a slave."
Art, age 10

" 'Let's have a truce. I forgive you because God has taught me how to forgive. You are my brothers and I love you.' . . . Then he started crying, and they all started crying too."
Mary, age 11

Speculation on the Spiritual Reason for Why God Brought the Entire Clan of Jacob and Joseph into Egypt

"The weather was better in Egypt. . . . That's why God brings so many people to places like Arizona now."
Herb, age 7

"I think they all just went there for Passover."
Adam, age 7

≈≈≈

"God was showing the people that life was complicated and that you had to work hard to get back to the Promised Land."
Peggy, age 10

VI

"Moses, when God gave you the Ten Commandments, were they really heavy to carry?"

(the Exodus story, from Egypt to the Promised Land)

he mere mention of the name Moses conjures images of unparalleled leadership, wisdom, and holiness. Pharaoh may have tried to strike the name from all records in the ancient lands, but Moses remains perhaps the grandest figure in the Old Testament. Possibly because of Moses' intimate and consequential conversations with God, initially through the miracle of the burning bush and then, more directly, on Mount Sinai, we have come to think of Moses as particularly close to God.

At the same time—and children learn this too—we are told that Moses is not a god but a person, great though he was. And therefore this saga about the Hebrews' flight from bondage is

more than a biography of Moses, but rather a historical paradigm of man's struggle against oppression and an illustration of the role that God plays in the pursuit of freedom. It is a story for all time and for all generations, at least as important for children as it is for adults. Here we learn that it is possible to move all the way from the

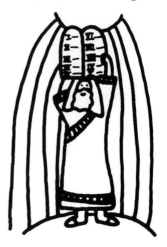

despair of slavery to a vision of the Promised Land, if we choose to fully embrace God and God's law. In this way, the Ten Commandments represent the ultimate lessons of life—a guide for living that can be understood as readily by the seven-year-old as by the seventy-year-old.

Why the Egyptians Enslaved Other People

~~~

"They had bad upbringings."
Sara L., age 9

~~~

"It was laziness. They wanted those pyramids to be perfect, but they didn't want to wear the hard helmets and do the work themselves."
Edgar, age 12

~~~

"I think they never took any lessons in manners, or no lessons in God either."
Mary Beth, age 7

On How Moses' Mother Saved Him from a Terrible Fate

~~~

"She wrote him an excuse so he didn't have to work on the pyramids."
Tally, age 9

"She made sure he ate wheat cereals instead of sugar cereals that were bad for him."
Lori Ann, age 8

～～～

"His mother made believe he was an Egyptian and so she taught him to say things like, 'May Isis bless you.' "
Lewis, age 11

～～～

"His mother dressed him up like an Egyptian so Moses could meet Egyptian girls later on."
Augie, age 7

～～～

"The Egyptians were after the Jewish kids, so she sent Moses along the river in a little rowboat. . . . She had to give him up, so it hurt a lot, but sometimes a mother has to let go."
Olivia, age 11

～～～

"She sent him away, and then I think he went to a private school and became an Egyptian leader or something."
Art, age 10

When He Grew Up, What Exactly Did Moses Look Like?

〜〜

"He walked like an Egyptian. . . . Like with his hands out and flat."
Toni, age 11

〜〜

"Moses was pretty handsome-looking. . . . He definitely didn't wear any earrings."
Leandra, age 10

〜〜

"Long hair and a headband that said FREEDOM FOR THE PEOPLE on it."
Kelly, age 10

〜〜

"Gray beard and gray hair. . . . He probably walked with a limp because of all the sand he got in his shoes from all the desert time he had to do."
Greg, age 11

〜〜

"Actually, Moses was a ninety-pound weakling and the Egyptians kicked dirt in his face. . . . But God did everything by pumping him up with faith."
Bob, age 12

The Important Words That the Voice from the Burning Bush Spoke to Moses While He Was in the Wilderness

"SHALOM, MOSES. . . . I HAVE A MISSION FOR YOU."
Carey, age 7

"MOSES, HAVE I GOT SOME COMMANDMENTS FOR YOU!
TEN, TO BE EXACT."
Art, age 10

"DON'T BE AFRAID OF ME. I AM THE LORD YOUR GOD.
SEE, I'M INVISIBLE. THAT'S HOW YOU CAN TELL FOR
SURE."
Neil, age 9

"HEY, MO, DO YOU KNOW ANY GOOD PLACES TO EAT
OUT HERE?"
Dick, age 7

"RELAX. . . . WHEN THE TIME IS RIGHT, MY BOY JESUS
IS GOING TO OPEN UP THE SEA FOR YOU."
Billie, age 10

"MOSES, TELL PHARAOH TO LET MY PEOPLE GO, AND
TELL HIM YOURS TRULY SENT YOU!"
Edward, age 12

~~~

"MOSES, IS THAT YOU? GOOD. I HAVE SOME FROGS
AND MOSQUITOES FOR PHARAOH'S HOUSE. I WANT
YOU TO DELIVER THEM FIRST CLASS."
Ernie Y., age 9

When Moses and His Brother, Aaron, Said, "Let the People Go," How Did Pharaoh Respond?

~~~

"He said that it wasn't going to happen, because he had an evil
reputation to keep up."
Laurie, age 9

~~~

"He got real mad and he told Moses and his brother that you
don't get elected to being a Pharaoh by being a pushover. . . .
You got to have thousands of slaves first."
Lilly, age 10

~~~

"He said he didn't believe in God and it would take the sea
opening up to convince him. . . . Famous last words."
Toni, age 11

The Miraculous "Tricks" God Equipped Moses with in Order to Show Pharaoh That Moses Had the Power of God with Him

≈

"Moses could make one of those triangle buildings disappear."
Lori Ann, age 8

≈

"God made Pharaoh have a heart-to-heart talk with a snake."
Charles, age 9

≈

"The Nile River got a change of color just like that. . . .
It was blood red."
Griffin, age 10

≈

"If everything else didn't work, Moses could have caused a
flood at Pharaoh's house and made the toilets overflow."
Liz, age 10

≈

"Moses turned a stick into a snake. But the biggest thing was
that he spoke the truth. But the truth isn't a trick, it's just an
important thing."
Kimberly, age 12

What the Ten Plagues Sought to Accomplish

"Convince the Pharaoh that he wasn't God's gift to the world."
Heather, age 10

"Show God's power so it would be easier to get people to obey the Ten Commandments later on."
Carey, age 7

Which One Was the Most Awful Plague?

"Dandruff."
Doug, age 8

"Frogs. . . . All that jumpin' around would get to me."
Wallace, age 9

"The worst was the plague about school."
Jimmy F., age 7

"I think it hailed and rained on them and they didn't have
umbrellas yet."
Anita D., age 9

"The first-born plague. . . . Killing is always an awful thing for
the world and God was probably sorry He had to do that."
Carey, age 7

How Did the Hebrew People Let the Angel of Death Know that He Should "Pass Over" Their Homes?

"Didn't they put a lamb on top of their roof?"
Julia, age 9

"Stars on their windows, and it said BEWARE OF THE DOG on the
front lawns."
Griffin, age 10

"The people just looked friendly and smiled a lot and asked the
angel how his kids were. . . . They were hoping he would like
them enough to let them go."
Charles, age 9

What Did Pharaoh Decide to Do After He Released the People?

"Become a Christian?"
Serena, age 9

"He cried, because he had got so used to them. It's hard not having millions of slaves around to do the laundry and make the buildings and things like that."
Sara L., age 9

"Told his ministers and helpers to get his chariot, because he wanted to look tough if he was going to lose to God."
Dean, age 10

"I think he went back on his word and tried to catch the people with his army, but the army showed they were no good at the Ironman Triathlon at the Red Sea."
Edward, age 12

The Far-out Means of Transportation the Hebrew People Used to Cross the Red Sea

"They let God take care of all their travelin' needs."
Ted, age 11

"There was a special lane for them. . . . I think the Egyptians got arrested for following them into the lane."
Dion, age 6

"They found an old ark that wasn't used in hundreds and hundreds of years."
Julia, age 9

"God let them walk on the water, but only for ten minutes."
Heidi, age 9

"God built them some walls in the sea and the people walked through like it was a tunnel."
Carey, age 7

Once They Were in the Desert Wilderness, How Did God Respond to the Hunger of the People?

"Food deliveries direct from the sky."
Carey, age 7

"God had an angel that was a good baker make dozens of soft breads for the people. . . . It might have been like that sourdough kind."
Nina, age 8

"He said, 'I know my people are hungry. Here, people, eat some granola. It's nutritious.' "
Larry G., age 9

"Yeah, they were hungry. So God fed them with loaves of bread and with fish. That's what his specialty is."
Chester, age 9

What Was the Special Food from Heaven Called and What Did It Taste Like?

≈

"Manna. . . . It tasted something like flavored cream cheese."
Barry, age 10

≈

"Communion. . . . People have been swallowin' ever since."
Philip, age 9

≈

"On Fridays, the people always got challah [Jewish bread] from heaven. . . . So they could celebrate the Sabbath."
Carey, age 7

≈

"Moses cakes. . . . Pretty much had the taste of rice cakes."
Sheila, age 9

What Happened on Mount Sinai?

≈

"There was a big ceremony and God passed a torch to Moses and Moses ran down the hill with it."
Thomas J., age 8

"The Ten Commandments got created and time stood still."
Toni, age 11

"I think Jesus visited there and he ran into Moses once in a while."
Dean, age 10

"I think that was the first time the world got some rules. . . . I think we need a lot more."
Robin, age 8

Ancient Journalist's Account of What Moses Said to God When He Received the Ten Commandments

"Moses was in tears when he saw the Commandments and he just kept saying, 'I'm sorry, I'm sorry. I broke number six last week.'"
Sandy, age 10

"This late word just in. Mark it down on your calendar. July 7, 1000 B.C. . . . Moses just got the Ten Commandments from God. His first words were: 'Can I talk it over with my lawyer first, sir?'"
Andrew, age 12

The One Commandment That Could Well Be the Most Important

~~~

"BE NICE AND FINISH YOUR SOUP. . . . That's a big one."
Tracy, age 4

~~~

"THOU SHOULD BE A GOOD PERSON. IT WON'T HURT YOU NONE."
Lonnie, age 8

~~~

"THOU MUST CHILL OUT AND DON'T HAVE ANY WARS."
Charles, age 9

~~~

"THOU SHALL NOT LIE. YOUR MOTHER AND GOD WILL FIND OUT THE TRUTH ANYWAYS."
Selena, age 11

~~~

"DEFINITELY LOVE YOUR NEIGHBOR LIKE IT WAS YOU THAT WAS LIVING NEXT DOOR."
Billie, age 10

What Did the Hebrew People Build When They Became Restless and Bored in the Wilderness?

"A stadium for sports?"
Derrick, age 8

"Condos."
Howie, age 8

"A gold animal they took from a jewelry store in Egypt."
Robin, age 8

"An idol to worship. That was stupid. People who build those never get to win in the Bible."
Heidi, age 9

"They built some kind of gold thing but then Moses and God found out and then it was all a big problem. . . . The people should have realized that you don't need to see something to believe in it."
Mark K., age 12

What Did Moses Do When He Saw the Golden Calf?

"He said to God, 'Maybe it's a good time for You to nap, God.' "
Fred, age 9

"Moses said, 'Aaron, my brother. You are a villain. Why did you let this happen? Mom was right about you.' "
Alexia, age 11

"He dropped the big Commandment tablets and then he needed some little tablets . . . the ones called aspirin."
Greg, age 11

"Moses almost leveled the first people he saw. Then he turned blue and he screamed, 'The calf goes or else we stay in the desert forever. What will it be, folks?' "
Edwin, age 10

After Forty Years in the Desert, and with Moses' Remaining Days but Few, What Did God Allow Moses to Do?

"See the Promised Land with a pair of old-fashioned binoculars."
Robin, age 8

"Taste food that was in the future . . . like sushi."
Peggy, age 10

"He could choose eternal youth if he wanted it, but Moses was more interested in a soft cloud in heaven."
Ricky, age 7

If You Could Have Been There with Moses During His Last Days, What One Question Would You Have Asked Him?

≈≈

"Moses, can I have that rod you used with the Pharaoh? The one you changed into a snake. . . . Is there a kid's replica of that?"

Ryan, age 10

≈≈

"Did your hair really turn white when you met God or was it just that way in the movie?"

Virginia, age 9

≈≈

"Moses, how did you really open up the Red Sea? What did God tell you to do so that the people didn't get wet?"

Carey, age 7

≈≈

"Can I keep the rocks from the Commandments you broke as a souvenir? Would you mind autographing them?"

Edgar, age 12

≈≈

"How well do you know Jesus? First-name basis?"

Greg, age 11

"Moses, when God gave you the Ten Commandments, were
they really heavy to carry?"
Rusty, age 9

What This Biblical Saga Teaches About the Human Condition and About Life in General

"Be patient. Sometimes good news takes forty years."
Sara L., age 9

"Go with God. It's a sure thing."
John C., age 8

"If you go to Egypt, only visit for a little while unless it's
changed a lot. . . . You could get stuck there for a long time."
Thomas J., age 8

"If you meet a Pharaoh or a bad guy and he bothers you, just
say the magic word: *plague*."
Edwin, age 10

"People aren't meant to be slaves, but they aren't gods either.
They're just people."
Molly, age 11

"Never give up hope. There could be a miracle waiting for you just around the corner."
Julia, age 9

〜〜

"All of God's children are trying to make it to the Promised Land, so try to clear a path for them so they can get through."
Andrew, age 12

VII

"Samson probably hated going to the barber like I do"

(the Samson and Delilah story)

ome Old Testament stories seem as mythological as they do religious. Such is the case with the story of Samson, the herculean figure who was felled by his enticing nemesis, Delilah, but then regained his strength and wreaked havoc on his Philistine adversaries. Against the backdrop of the themes of trust and betrayal, the story paradoxically turns on a most physical, yet spiritual, factor: the length of Samson's hair, which was the source of his God-given prowess. Children find this element charming and intriguing, and humorous too, as they speculate on the meaning of the theological events and on the quirky and ill-fated relationship of Samson and Delilah.

The Famous Israelite Who Would Not Cut His Hair and the Reason Why He Wouldn't Cut It

≈≈

"Samson. . . . He wouldn't cut it because it was in style in his day, like it was in the 1960s."
Vickie, age 11

≈≈

"I forget his name, but I think he wouldn't cut it because God told him not to, and he cared more about what God thought than if people said he was a slob."
Tyrone, age 10

≈≈

"That guy didn't get a haircut because it would have ended his wrestling career."
Grant, age 8

≈≈

"The hair gave Samson strength. He didn't even have to work out hard or pump iron. All he had to do was grow the hair."
Darius, age 9

≈≈

"Samson probably hated going to the barber like I do, and that's what got him into so much trouble."
Ethan, age 7

What Were Some of the Feats of Strength for Which Samson Was Renowned?

~~~

"Ten thousand push-ups in an hour. . . . And he could pray at the same time."
Ross, age 10

~~~

"Samson could lift chariots like they were kids' bicycles."
Clint, age 8

~~~

"I think he fought lions and tigers but he told them to start out on top of him just so *they* had a chance."
Derrick, age 8

~~~

"He took apart some temple when he was already old and retired. . . . I can't remember if he put the pillars back together."
Angela, age 10

Why Do You Think God Gives Some People Special Gifts, Such as the Strength God Gave to Samson?

"It's the only way He can get anybody to take piano lessons. . . . God gives them the gift of music talent first."
Marti, age 9

"It's to do good things in the world and to make sure there's somebody around who is strong enough to open tight lids and stuff."
Joey, age 6

"Everybody has special things from God. Not just Samson. It's up to us to figure out what it is, and you got to know how to use it."
Judy, age 11

"I don't know how it happens, but if you have to end up blind like Samson did, then I wouldn't want one of those special gifts."
Andrew, age 12

Introducing That Woman Named Delilah, and Her Dastardly Deed

"Delilah was a dish. I saw her in an old movie."
Denny, age 9

"I think she was a traitor like Judas was later on. . . . They just kinda pop up on you in the Bible."
Marti, age 9

"She probably ate food that wasn't kosher. . . .
That was a big no-no."
Gabriel, age 10

"Samson got his hair cut because Delilah was jealous of his curly hair. . . . His hair was much nicer than hers."
Sheila, age 9

"She was the wrong kind of girlfriend to have . . . the kind that tries to tell you that you should change how you look."
Tyrone, age 10

"I think she was just confused. She was too young
for him anyways."
Beth, age 5

What Did Samson Say When He Realized His Great Locks Had Been Trimmed?

"There goes my gig on MTV! . . . Everybody on that station
has long hair."
Andrew, age 12

"Oh, no, I'm bald! . . . Have hairclubs for men been
invented yet?"
Brett, age 11

"Where has all my power gone? Gee, I need God to recharge
me. . . . Maybe now He can put the strength in my eyebrows."
Diana, age 12

After He Had Lost His Strength and He Was Blinded and Imprisoned, What Did Samson Request of God?

≋

"He wanted God to make sure Delilah got punished. He didn't want anything too mean, just something like starving and her hair falling out."
Angela, age 10

≋

"Samson just wanted one more chance to take a club and hit a home run with a couple of the Philistines."
Andrew, age 12

≋

"He begged God to give him his strength back. I think that he was real hung up on being strong and being a he-man."
Jody, age 8

Samson's Revenge: What Did He Do to Punish the Philistines for Their Cruelty?

≋

"He called them 'Philly Sissies.'"
Albert, age 8

"Samson got some extra vitamins and he was able to knock down their buildings."
Philip, age 9

≋

"I think he broke down a big house where they were all playing blackjack."
Barry, age 10

≋

"With the extra muscles God gave him, Samson knocked down the pillars of the temple. . . . All the people inside got killed, but don't feel sorry for them, because they should have thought about what they were doing when they acted like big morons."
Hannah, age 9

What, if Anything, the Samson and Delilah Story Says About the Relationship Between the Sexes

≋

"Some men and some ladies are good people, but if you meet a phony one of either kind, don't let them give you a haircut."
Zalman, age 9

≋

"Bad relationships can be murder on your hair."
Jenny, age 12

"Be careful about ladies with funny names like Delilah and Delulu. . . . Stay with ones with simple names like Debbie."
Austin, age 8

~~

"Learn what Samson learned: just because you can move big pillars don't mean that you are ready for a serious relationship. You got to be real mature for that."
Rodney, age 9

VIII

"David hit that big Goliath with his secret weapon, and the giant went down for the count"

(the legacy of the great King David, including his battle with Goliath and the contributions of his son, Solomon)

**W**henever we come across situations in life where an outcome seems preordained, where an overriding favorite is paired against a little-known and decided underdog, the story of David and Goliath comes to mind. This biblical confrontation had been passed down to generations of children as the prototypical example of victory against all odds, and as an exemplar of the power of faith and intelligence over sheer brawn and physical dominance. The vision of the slender David, the boy who would be king, loading his slingshot and preparing it for battle against the mammoth Goliath, is a compelling one for children of many different religious backgrounds.

But of course there was more to David's legacy than his improbable battlefield upset, as earth-shattering as it was. Together with the reign of his offspring and successor, Solomon, David's kingship is also worth remembering. This was a time of considerable prestige for the Hebrew people, an era of military clout, impressive temples, and the lasting con-

tributions of biblical literature, as embodied by David's Psalms and Solomon's Proverbs. Such richness offers youngsters much to learn and interpret, with divinely inspired wisdom as bountiful as the fruit and breads on the tables of a king's palace.

When It Came to Pass That the Judge Named Samuel Foretold That the Boy David Would Someday Be King, What Is the Boy Reported to Have Said?

"Can I have this promise in writing, Mr. Samuel?"
Terry N., age 11

"King? But I wanted to be a dancer or a musician."
Heidi, age 9

"How can I be king? I'm only ten! I'm only in the fourth grade!"
Norm, age 9

"How can I be sure that you are right? Did Someone invisible tell you this? Was He real powerful and did He talk out of a wind or a fire?"
Connie, age 10

"Please don't rush me, sir. . . . I haven't even been bar mitzvahed yet."
Seth, age 12

"The next thing you are going to telling me is that a skinny kid like me is going to be a great warrior too.... That'll be the day!"
Vickie, age 11

For What Cultural Purpose Was Young David Summoned to King Saul's Palace?

"To play some fast tunes on his harp."
Reuben, age 10

"To paint the chapel some bright colors and get people to go to religious services more."
Rodney, age 9

"Saul was real angry all the time and he needed to hear some cool music, and David's group was, like, having a tour and so they called him."
Amy, age 9

Given His Cultural Interests, What Moved Young David to Become a Warrior and Enter Battle with the Philistine Behemoth, Goliath?

〰️

"God gave him the courage to do it. Without God, he would have been just a regular kid."
Robin, age 8

〰️

"Goliath was calling the Jews names so somebody had to stand up to him. After it was over, Goliath wasn't calling anybody names no more."
Charles, age 9

〰️

"It was one of those things you had to do before you could become the king. . . . The other things were, like, hunting animals and having five wives."
Meghan, age 9

What Was the Secret, Unlikely Weapon That David Brought to the Battle with Goliath?

"Sunflower seeds. . . . It gave him extra strength."
Ethan, age 7

"When David went to fight Goliath, he definitely had a Star of David with him."
Gabriel, age 10

"David probably carried a spare slingshot with him. You can never tell when you might get in an accident and sit on your good one."
Charles, age 9

Eyewitness Comments from Battlefield Spectators After David Defeated Goliath

"You know that every kid in the country is going to want a slingshot now, and the price is going to go up."
Charles, age 9

"David hit that big Goliath with his secret weapon, and the giant went down for the count."
Art, age 10

≈≈

"Did you see those shields? Those were awesome. It shows what modern technology can do. I'm glad our tax money isn't wasted."
Bert, age 7

≈≈

"I didn't even know there was going to be a fight between David David and Goliath Jones. . . . I was just here because I heard there was an Elvis sighting."
Lauren, age 12

≈≈

"That David sure is handsome. . . . I'm going to see if he'll autograph my T-shirt."
Lacy, age 9

What the Battle of David and Goliath Symbolizes

≈≈

"Good guys do win, even regular people like farmers and shepherds and boys with slingshots."
Vickie, age 11

"Good is better than bad. . . . It really is."
Marianne, age 7

"Young people are good at things too. . . . You can tell that God picked David because He was going with a youth movement at the time."
Ross, age 10

"Size don't matter as long as you have fighting spirit and a few good rocks with you."
Ernie N., age 8

How Did David Eventually Become a King?

"He won it in a chariot race for charity."
Greg, age 11

"I think that David just knew the right people."
Theresa, age 8

"He fought more battles and he went undefeated."
Robbie T., age 10

"God made sure he got to be king. . . . God's will gets done."
Geoffrey, age 12

~~~

"He might have won an election. Everybody knew about him from when he beat the big ogre and then he probably made a lot of speeches and promises."
Marti, age 9

Psalm Wisdom from King David (Psalm 23):

"The Lord is my shepherd . . ."

~~~

"And He's so mighty he can make the sheep talk and dance if He wants to."
Serena, age 9

~~~

"The Lord is my shepherd. I like Him. But I don't always like the rest of the flock of sheep."
Andrew, age 12

~~~

"He is my favorite shepherd and Jesus is my favorite fisherman."
Leandra, age 10

Psalm Wisdom from King David, continued (Psalm 23):

"Yea, though I walk through the valley of the shadow of death . . ."

≈≈

"I'm not ready to die because I want to visit Florida, so I'm going to ask God for another five years."
Ted, age 11

≈≈

"Though I am walking through the valley of death, I'm not afraid because I'm walking on my tippy-toes so no one can hear me."
Loren, age 11

≈≈

"Death isn't going to touch me because I can run real fast in these sneakers. . . . And I ought to, because they sure cost a lot."
Dean, age 10

≈≈

"I can make it through that valley because I know God is on the other side."
Lewis, age 11

In His Later Years, What Advice Do You Suppose King David Gave to the Heir to His Throne, His Son, Solomon

"Son, just have one wife. . . . That's all a man can handle."
Cheryl, age 12

"Read a lot, Solomon. Don't dare think that you know it all."
Danny, age 9

"Don't press your luck and try out a giant in battle like I did."
Meghan, age 9

"Be a wise king, Solomon, and make the people think you are running a democracy."
Corwin, age 9

As Solomon Continued to Grow Up, How Did He Get to Be So Wise?

"Reader's Digest."
Elliot, age 11

"Maybe he read a lot by the fireplace, like President Lincoln did."

Tyrone, age 10

≈≋≈

"He went to the King School and he had a big king diploma on his wall at the temple."

Philip, age 9

≈≋≈

"I think maybe he stayed up late and memorized the Bible, or at least as much as was written down till then. He probably never dreamed that he would be in it someday."

Bert, age 7

When Solomon Was Faced with That Memorable Incident in Which Two Women Each Claimed to Be the Mother of the Same Baby Boy, How Did He Decide Between Them?

≈≋≈

"He asked which one of them liked boys better and which one didn't mind changing diapers."

Diana, age 12

"The one that came the closest to guessing the baby's weight got the baby. . . . And then they got to go for the grand prize too."
Lewis, age 11

≋

"He did eeny-meeny-miney-mo."
Shelly, age 6

≋

"Solomon made a quick call to God and asked for the true answer as quick as an angel could bring the message down."
Harry, age 9

≋

"Solomon decided to test the love of the mothers by acting like he was going to cut the baby in half. . . . It was a disgusting idea but it worked good."
Andrew, age 12

Titles of Some of Solomon's Books

≋

"The Book of Proverbs and Ideas You Can Really Use at Home."
Andrew, age 12

≋

"How to Be Wise: In Ten Easy Steps."
Joel, age 12

"Solomon's Book of Royal Cats."
Nicki, age 7

"Solomon's View of God: It's Written by the Popular King Himself."
Connie, age 10

What Was the Greatest and Grandest Accomplishment in the Days of King David and King Solomon?

"Biggest temple without elevators."
Leandra, age 10

"David's Cookies. They were the first cookies that actually had a name."
Howie, age 8

"They wrote the most prayers ever. . . . I think it's really important to say good prayers."
Cynthia, age 9

"Neither kings raised taxes or charged people for stamps. That don't happen much with kings back then or now either."
Britt, age 10

IX

"God made the whale burp and out came Jonah"

(the misfortunes of Daniel, Jonah, and Job)

Like everyday life, the Old Testament is full of predicaments—difficult and perplexing situations that require resolution or escape and demand that the hero acquire some new insight and perspective on life. The biblical quagmires are often dire and dangerous, and the most famous of these are the three stories that are featured in this chapter.

Daniel in the lion's den and Jonah and the whale are both adventure-story predicaments in which the main character encounters life-threatening creatures of nature. But through faith and understanding—and, above all, as a result of God's personal intervention—both the pious Daniel and the more rebellious Jonah are spared and bear witness to the ways of the Lord. Children embrace these colorful stories because of their action and simple plots, not to mention the curious behavior of the lions and the whale. The youngsters are also enraptured because the stories convey to us that even in precarious situations, we can find comfort and safety in our belief in the protective nature of God.

The story of Job is also a predicament that concentrates on issues of faith, but it is far more enigmatic for children—as well as for adults. Often grouped with the wisdom literature of the

Bible, the Book of Job provides a great springboard for discussion about the relationship between God and ourselves. Children express great interest in the appearance of Satan in this story too, as they grapple with this embodiment of evil and sin. Thus, Job's dilemma represents an excellent window into the nature of good and evil and how children perceive each.

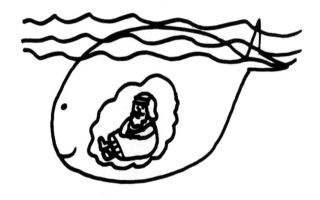

Daniel in the Lion's Den

In the Time of the Babylonian Captivity, a Man Named Daniel Read the Handwriting That Mysteriously Appeared on the Palace Wall, and the Message Read:

≈

"JUST DO IT. . . . I'M TALKING ABOUT PRAYING, NOT PLAYING
BASKETBALL."
Tyrone, age 10

≈

"CINDY LOVES DANIEL. . . . SIGNED CINDY."
Gerri, age 7

≈

"NO SMOKING IN THE PALACE. GOD SAYS IT'S BAD FOR OUR HEALTH."
Connie, age 10

≈

"I KNOW IT MUST FEEL FUNNY TO READ A WALL, BUT I HAD TO FIND
A WAY TO GET YOUR ATTENTION. DON'T BE SLAVES TO NOBODY. I
DIDN'T CREATE YOU ALL TO BE TREATED LIKE ANIMALS."
Abby, age 9

"The message wasn't on the wall, it was on the ceiling. It said: LOOK UP HERE. I AM THE LORD YOUR GOD. YEAH, I'M THE REAL THING."
Armand, age 12

"ROSES ARE RED, VIOLETS ARE BLUE, THIS IS A MAGIC WALL, AND IT SAYS GOD LOVES YOU."
Cheryl, age 12

Why Was Daniel Soon Thrown into a Lion's Den?

"His hunting was hurting the lion population. A nature group told on him."
Sondra, age 7

"He said the emperor wasn't wearing any clothes."
Bobby, age 8

"It was probably 'cuz he was Jewish. . . . It used to happen a lot to them."
Corwin, age 9

"Daniel spelled *lion* wrong and the government there was real tough on spelling."
Kerry T., age 7

What Advice Did the King Give Daniel When He Had Daniel Placed in the Lion's Den?

"Your best chance is if you tell the lions some jokes. . . . Lions have a good sense of humor."
Lori Ann, age 8

"Now is when that track-running experience is going to come in handy."
Carl, age 10

"Daniel, dress up in a ringmaster's uniform and maybe they will obey you."
Eric, age 9

"Just hope they already ate dinner."
Ethan, age 7

"After it's all over, come back as an angel and say hello."
Clare, age 10

"Hebrew, remember that your God loves to help out in lost causes like yours."
Thomas L., age 11

Possible Prayers Uttered by Daniel as the Lions Approached

~~~

"God, there isn't time for a long prayer. So I'll just say 'HELP'
and I know you will get the message."
Howie, age 8

~~~

"Please forgive my sins and make the lions have good hearts."
Margaret, age 6

~~~

"Dear God, please make the lions' teeth fall out real fast.
Amen."
Dani, age 7

~~~

"Heavenly Father . . . I'm in a little trouble and it's going to
take a miracle to get me out of this one."
Clare, age 10

As a Result of Daniel's Abiding Faith, What Did God Do to Insure Daniel's Safety?

"The lions were forced to smile at Daniel and rub up against his nose."
Toshi, age 10

"God kept the lions away from Daniel by showing them pictures of girl lions."
Andrew, age 12

"He fed the lions good first so they didn't turn Daniel into chop suey. . . . It's a good thing that lions don't eat dessert or it could have been Danny."
Anthony, age 9

"I think he made the lions like kitty cats by closing their mouths. . . . All they could do was say 'meow.' "
Connie, age 10

"Right there on the spot, God taught those lions the meaning of friendship."
Sheila, age 9

What the Relieved Daniel May Have Said after He Was Released from the Den

≈≈

"Thank God. . . . Praise the Lord. . . . Now that I'm free,
I'm going to Disneyworld."
Jay, age 9

≈≈

"I'm still sweating. Whew, that was rough. After being in
that lion's den, I think I'm never going to take my kids to
the zoo again."
Sheila, age 9

The Time-Honored Moral Lessons of the Story of Daniel and the Lions

≈≈

"Keep away from lions that don't believe in God."
Alison, age 7

≈≈

"If you start talking to lions, it doesn't mean you're going
batty. . . . It could be God is up to something."
Carmen, age 8

Jonah and the Whale

In the Land of Nineveh, What Did God Ask a Man Named Jonah to Do That Jonah Tried to Avoid Doing?

〜〜

"God wanted him to be Jonah of Ark, but Jonah didn't really
want the fame and all the trouble that goes with it."
Luke, age 10

〜〜

"Jonah didn't want to get to the city of Ninnies and warn them
that God was ticked off at them for having no religion."
Greg, age 11

〜〜

"Jonah was supposed to be a prophet but he was only
interested in fishing and money profits."
Andrew, age 12

〜〜

"God wanted Jonah to go to Gilligan's Island and save some
stowaways."
Nellie, age 11

How It Came to Be That the Ship That Jonah Boarded Encountered So Many Difficulties

~~~

"A whale was playing with the boat like it was a
toy boat in a bathtub."
Howie, age 8

~~~

"The hull of the boat didn't move good because God was
holding it back with His arms. . . . I think God was there
because He was out there fishing."
Corwin, age 9

~~~

"God called over to a whale to ram it a few times until Jonah
popped into the air and landed in the whale's mouth like he
was a little salty peanut."
Lewis, age 11

~~~

"There was a big storm and the sailors knew they were cursed
because they had Jonah on board. . . . That's when they
decided he was sort of extra cargo."
Ross, age 10

When He Found Himself in the Belly of the Mighty Whale, What Did Jonah Do?

"He drew a calendar inside the whale's stomach and marked off
the days he was there."
Camille, age 10

"Jonah wished that he was already in Heaven instead of inside
the whale, because the whale had indigestion problems."
Sara L., age 9

"He made friends with a man from Africa who came sailin' in."
Tyrone, age 10

"Jonah prayed for help, and he promised God that if he ever
got out of there, he would be a whale of a good guy."
Edward, age 12

What Is the Real Story Behind How Jonah Eventually Escaped?

≈

"God made the whale burp and out came Jonah."
Becky, age 8

≈

"Jonah used a hammer and the whale started laughing because it tickled, and that's when Jonah took off."
Howie, age 8

≈

"The whale spitted Jonah out because he tasted no good. . . . He wasn't what the whale liked. The whale liked tuna."
Kerry P., age 7

≈

"God gave the whale heartburn and the whale had to open his mouth, and Jonah got a free ride on a piece of tree that he made into a raft."
Lonnie, age 8

Concerning What Jonah Learned About God's Ways from This Whale Episode

"God knows what is for our own good."
Mike, age 8

"Wear a life jacket. . . . You can't expect God to save you all the time if you go overboard."
Robin, age 8

"Pray every single day, because the Lord is sure here to stay."
Mark P., age 10

"Jonah learned mostly about whales. He learned that whales are not good to visit and pet. Even if you can get in free."
Nancy P., age 6

The Hard-to-Understand Story of Job

Debating with the Devil: What Satan Said to God About a Decent Man Named Job

≈≈≈

"In my not-so-humble opinion, God, Job is a nerd for
worshipping you."
Andrew, age 12

≈≈≈

"Just give me five minutes with that Job guy. . . .
I'll get him sinning."
Terry N., age 11

≈≈≈

"Please give me the Job job."
Greg, age 11

≈≈≈

"Big G, I want that man off the earth by sundown. I can't
stand perfect people."
Howie, age 8

Why Do You Think Job Was Singled Out for a Test of Spiritual Faith?

〜〜

"Job might have sent in a postcard with his name on it and then he got to be the one."
Thomas J., age 8

〜〜

"God wouldn't let that mean Satan guy pick on a lady or any children. . . . It had to be a grown-up man like Job."
Ethan, age 7

〜〜

"Maybe he was just next in line. That's how teachers do it. They go by who is next. Maybe God does it like that too."
Cathy, age 6

〜〜

"I think he was rich and he had it good. So they were trying to see what would happen if he had troubles. . . . But faith isn't something you can take away that easy."
Toni, age 11

The Terrible Things That Befell Job

〜〜

"Blindness and bad business deals."
Lewis, age 11

"His crops wouldn't grow, and what made it worse was that he was a farmer."
Kim C., age 8

"He got robbed by somebody wearing a Frankenstein mask."
Daniel, age 6

"He got headaches all the time and there was no headache medicine back then."
Jay, age 9

"Job got really sad and he didn't even know why. Nobody could cheer him up. Even the funny get-well cards didn't work."
Sheila, age 9

When, After These Calamities, Job Found Himself in a Whirlwind, What Explanation Did God Offer Him?

"Why are you complaining? You're ungrateful! What have you ever done? Ever create a whole planet?"
Toni, age 11

"You know, you remind Me of a fellow named Noah. He was a nuisance too. I almost changed My mind about leaving him out of the flood."
Ross, age 10

"Look, Job, everybody has off days. . . . Well, everybody except Me."
Diana, age 12

"Don't question My ways. . . . You don't know that much, even if you have a fancy education!"
Arlene, age 10

Based on the Story of Job, How Can We Explain the Relationship Between God and Satan?

"God is like my mother and the Devil is like my little brother."
Austin, age 8

"God is the boss of the world and Satan is like a thief that is trying to steal everything the world owns."
Tyrone, age 10

"They used to be related to each other but then there was a family problem."
Peter F., age 9

"One is totally good and the other doesn't bother tryin'."
Ernie N., age 8

"God prints books like the Bible and sometimes He has to make up characters like Satan. Most of the people in the Bible are real, but Satan isn't, he's a made-up idea. He's just there to show how you shouldn't act."
Clare, age 10

Lasting Lessons from the Book of Job

"All wisdom comes from God. It is not our place to reason why, we should just do and try."
Caitlin, age 12

"Evil does exist, and it's real tricky. . . . Let God take care of it. You should stay away from it."
Cynthia, age 9

"You should be enjoying what you have because it's hard to predict what will happen next in life."
Diana, age 12

≈

"You might have to go through some small troubles or even big troubles so you can learn what you need to know."
Terry B., age 8

≈

"God made the earth and the sun, but He really did save what He cares about most for last. . . . That's us. . . . He loves us and we should love Him no matter what is happening around us."
Melanie, age 11

"The Bible is the best book ever written because it has the most creative Author"

(reflections on the Old Testament)

o read the Old Testament is to enter into some of the richest stories ever told. Out of the many challenges to the Hebrew people in the ancient world, and through their noteworthy patriarchs, kings, and prophets chosen by God, we are able to follow along with our children and trace the early roots of many religions and belief systems. Given the importance of the Old Testament in world history, it is interesting to see how children appraise these stories as a whole, and whether they comprehend the role of Bible stories in their own lives today.

Thus, we conclude our discussion with a summary of children's views on this great library of writings, as we move from our favorite Bible scenes and characters to the underlying messages of the Old Testament, to an explanation of why the Bible might aptly be called "the greatest book ever written."

Our Favorite Old Testament Stories

"I like the stories about the kings the best. . . . I always wanted to be one, and they don't have too many kings around anymore."
Barry, age 10

"The one with the guy and the colored coat is good. . . . I can relate to it because I have trouble with brothers too."
Andy, age 8

"David and Goliath is good because it has good weapons and a lot of action and you can cheer and stuff when the giant falls down."
Coleman, age 9

"When God made the sun and the birds and the creatures, that was amazing. . . . I would like to see that all in slow motion."
Howie, age 8

"I wish I could figure out dreams like some of the Bible people did. Then I would be the smartest kid in my class. Maybe in the whole school."
Jim, age 8

"I like how the first people were born. It says in the Bible that Adam came from dirt and Eve was created from Adam's rib. . . . Boy, that was a rough way to do it, so I'm sure glad God doesn't make girls like He used to. . . . It's a good thing."
Larry G., age 9

Which Old Testament Figure Most Reminds You of Yourself?

"Delilah. . . . I'm good at cutting hair too."
Clare, age 10

"There's a guy in it named Enoch. He isn't famous and neither am I."
Ernest, age 12

"Basically, any angel would be a good fit."
Gabriel, age 10

"I would say Jacob is like me a little because I like to wrestle and I like to travel. . . . But you wouldn't catch me sleeping on any stones."
Greg, age 11

"I could be a little like Eve because I like to eat apples a lot. . . . But I would have listened more to God than she did."
Marla, age 7

"Noah. . . . Maybe 'cuz he was organized and I'm pretty good at that, and I'm good at building big things too."
Coleman, age 9

"It sure isn't Satan. . . . I get in trouble sometimes, but I ain't *that* bad!"
Robert L., age 8

What Is the Overriding Message of the Old Testament?

"There is only one true God, just like it says on the tablets."
Roger, age 9

"God is great and people are pretty nice too."
Robin, age 8

"Life is really pretty simple: do good, don't do bad."
Gayle L., age 10

"Never eat apples right off a tree like Adam and Eve did, because that little fruit might get you into big trouble, or else worms might be calling it 'home.' "
Bert, age 7

∿∿

"Don't be a bad boy or girl. You should listen to God or you might end up in a whale."
Francis, age 7

∿∿

"The whole book is about what we shouldn't do and what we should do, and what choices we should make. . . . It's not a mystery book really, it's a book about real things."
Carla, age 10

∿∿

"The big message is to have faith. Later on they let you know a savior is going to come and that he is going to clean up all the problems and mistakes in the world."
Dennis, age 12

The View of God as Described in the Old Testament

∿∿

"Friendly . . . but kinda tough on atheists."
Julia, age 9

"Real busy. . . . He's in charge of people, animals, angels, oceans, and pretty much everything else."
Ethan, age 7

〜〜

"God is just a very powerful dude, but He loves all of His children and we love Him."
Art, age 10

〜〜

"God was the type that was real quick to make sure that the bad guys get out of town. . . . Like Clint Eastwood."
Andrew, age 12

〜〜

"He is real smart and good. God just seems like He is making the world as nice a place as possible, and He likes to make it real colorful too."
Sheila, age 9

Judging from the Old Testament, How Does God Seem to Communicate with People?

〜〜

"He used to do it through storms, but I think He's more quiet now."
Adam, age 7

"God talked to people in their hearts."
Cherie, age 7

≈≈

"God loves to travel with the wind and sometimes He came to
the people as the wind. . . . He's flexible that way."
Laurie, age 9

≈≈

"God comes in the silence and He gives people different
feelings they need. . . . Like I'm not afraid of mice anymore
because God gave me a not-afraid feeling."
Wayne, age 7

≈≈

"Mountains, bushes, animals, floods. . . . You name it, God used
it to get the message to the people."
Camille, age 10

What Does the Old Testament Suggest Is the Main Goal We Should All Be Striving For?

≈≈

"To get our heads and feet out of the sand and go find the
Promised Land."
Carl, age 10

"You should try to be one heck of a good person."
Ryan, age 10

≈≈

"Don't be a judge of people by how they look, but judge them
by how they are on the inside. . . . Like, David was just a kid
but he was pretty strong on the inside."
Keith T., age 9

≈≈

"Just try to be a happy normal person who loves God. . . .
Don't try to own your own army or something like that."
Wendy, age 10

≈≈

"Love God 365 days a year. . . . Be careful not to take many
days off."
Sheila, age 9

≈≈

"Be a peacemaker. . . . Blessed are the peacemakers."
Andrew, age 12

On Why the Bible Is Called "The Greatest Book Ever Written"

≈≈

"It has the most words and the smartest words."
Woody, age 7

"All the stories are good ones. There aren't any
that make you sleepy."
Howie, age 8

"The Bible is the best book ever written because it has the
most creative Author."
Cheryl, age 12

"The modern books don't say enough about morals in them
and the Bible has them topped on that by far."
Christine, age 10

"The Bible is just good for your soul."
Art, age 10

"You can get more direction from it than anything else I can
think of."
Diana, age 12

About the Author

Dr. David Heller is a leading authority on children and their views of religion and the world. He is the author of a number of successful books on the subject, including *The Best Christmas Presents Are Wrapped in Heaven, My Mother Is the Best Gift I Ever Got, Love Is Like a Crayon Because It Comes in All Colors, Talking to Your Child About God, The Soul of a Man, Dear God: Children's Letters to God,* and *The Children's God.* His work with children has been featured all across the country—in segments on *20/20* as well as on CNBC and numerous local television programs; in articles in *People, Parents, Good Housekeeping, Redbook, Catholic Digest, USA Today, Psychology Today,* and *Parenting;* and in nationally syndicated pieces for Universal Press Syndicate. His books have been translated into nine languages.

Dr. Heller's personal background is ecumenical. He is the son of a Holocaust survivor and grew up in an observant Jewish family, yet he was also one of the first Jewish students at a Jesuit Catholic high school in Connecticut. He graduated *summa cum laude* from Harvard and received his doctorate from the University of Michigan, where he did his dissertation on children and their religious beliefs about God. He has also taught at both Harvard and Michigan.

Dr. Heller lives in Boston with his wife, Elizabeth, who has coauthored several books with him.